Wandering in
Wiveliscombe
Discover the town in two
—— guided walks ——

*Welcome to
Wivey*

Bruce + Kim

Wandering in
Wiveliscombe
Discover the town in two
—— guided walks ——

Susan Maria Farrington
and
Graham Mark

COLDEN PUBLICATIONS
2012

First published 2012
Colden Publications
P O Box 22, Wiveliscombe
Somerset TA4 2ZH

© Susan Maria Farrington
  and Graham Mark

Designed and Typeset
in Helvetica Neue LT by
Legend Design
Yeovil, Somerset BA22 8RL

Printed by
Short Run Press Limited
Exeter, Devon EX2 7LW

British Library Cataloguing-in-Publication Data
A CIP record for this title is available from the
British Library

ISBN 978-0-9540992-2-0

Contents

for
Dixon Luxton

To write in verse of dear old Wilscombe town
Befits the pen of one more wise than I,
So if the thoughts expressed should bring a frown,
I pray you reader, kindly pass them by.

Chas. Collard, 11th November 1936

Preface

Revd Hancock in 1910

Wiveliscombe is fortunate in that, since the start of the 20th century when *Wifela's Combe* was published by Reverend Frederick Hancock (1848-1920), the town has been well documented, both by the written word and, more recently, in electronic format. We both worked with the team who were privileged to produce *Wiveliscombe: A History of a Somerset Market Town* in 2005, a project which highlighted the thriving interest in our local history. Since then it has become apparent that a concise, more portable handbook might be welcome, an adjunct to the highly popular town walks led for some years by local historian Dixon Luxton and, latterly, by the Somerset County Archaeologist Bob Croft, both Wiveliscombe residents.

Although a less comprehensive work, we hope this little guide to the town will answer questions and provide interest to both long-term residents, and those new to, or just visiting, Wiveliscombe. We are lucky to live in a lively and friendly community, and we hope that you will respect residents' privacy as you seek out the places of interest that have been highlighted. Please share in our enthusiasm for this unique corner of West Somerset as you unravel some of the past during these two walks, each of which will take about two hours, starting and finishing in The Square.

We are fortunate to have as sources a number of 19th century property sale catalogues and other archival material in the Somerset Heritage Centre. These are complemented by personal anecdotes and 'facts' which reflect differing memories. If our interpretation of these has erred, we crave forgiveness and ask that you let us know so that errors are not perpetuated.

SMF and GDM
Wiveliscombe
2012

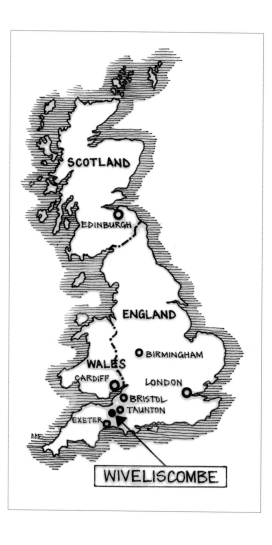

WIVELISCOMBE

Historic Context

In the distant prospect ... the blue hills in the sun shine stood out in bold relief around the valley of Taunton Deane. The Quantocks forming the horizon to the left, the Blackdowns to the right, and the eye strained towards the east could discover the high ground in Dorsetshire looming thro' the distance and bounding the rich and fertile landscape. There is no view on a fine clear afternoon in our neighbourhood so extensive and magnificent as this extending across the richest valley in Somersetshire.

Although un-attributed, this 19th century description of the town still holds good today. Wiveliscombe is blessed with its location at the foot of the Brendon Hills; although the centre has evolved, much that can be seen today would be recognised by a time traveller from the 19th century. From The Square four roads radiate out, while the medieval settlement and Bishop's manor are further to the south. New developments have taken place on three sides but, with the exception of Croft Way, there has been no new road construction.

There have been Neolithic and Bronze Age finds at Whitefield and Maundown in the north of the parish and there is an impressive Iron Age hill fort at Castle, to the east. South of the Taunton Road the Romans built a fort, a scheduled monument, which was partially excavated in 1956.

William Knight, Bishop 1541-47

From 1065, a year prior to the Norman Conquest, the parish was owned by the Bishops of Wells (later Bath & Wells). Their 13th century manor house, south-east of the Parish Church, was in regular use until confiscated by Queen Elizabeth in 1585. The Crown then leased the estate to the Coventry family, who were absentee landlords. Throughout, the town was administered by a Reeve and a Court Leet.

Upon the Crown lease expiring in 1820, the Bishop, Richard Beadon, regained possession of the parish. After his death in 1824, the estate was sold by his successor in 1827 to Bishop Beadon's son Richard. The properties were sold again in 1834 largely to Alexander Baring (1774-1848), of Barings Bank, MP for Taunton 1806-26 (created Lord Ashburton in 1835). He and his descendants held the lordship of the manor until 1894.

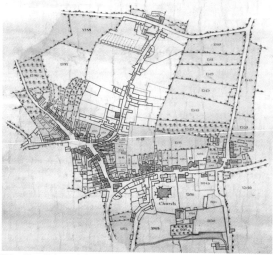

WIVELISCOMBE TOWN *ENLARGED*

Extract from Episcopal plan, 1816

Throughout the ages, the town has been the focus and market centre for the surrounding areas and the Brendon Hills. The main industry was the woollen trade which was declining by the early 1800s, to be replaced by new employment opportunities created by the Hancock brewery which began in 1806. The town flourished throughout the 19th century, in part by the arrival of the railway in 1871, and the adoption of the sport of rugby football, both of which had a major influence on the populace. The most significant building projects in the 19th century were the replacement of the parish church (1829), the 'Town Hall' (1842) in The Square, the latter commissioned by Lord Ashburton, and the development of the Hancock brewery buildings. In 1881, William Hancock II (1810-96) completed the dominant Court House as his family home, also in The Square. When the 4th Lord Ashburton needed to raise capital in 1894, he sold the Wiveliscombe estate and many of the tenants took the opportunity to purchase their premises.

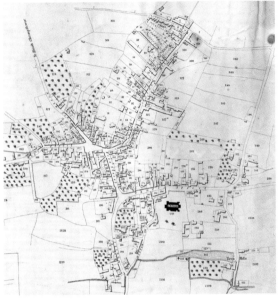

Map of town (1841)

After administrative changes brought in by Act of Parliament in 1894, the civil parish, which has similar boundaries to the ecclesiastic parish, comprised the town of Wiveliscombe (182 acres) and Wiveliscombe Without (5,803 acres). These were merged in 1986, and the Parish Council meets monthly throughout the year. From a figure of 1,500 in 1777, the population grew to c.3,000 in 1871 before declining to c.2,000 after the 1914-18 War. It remained at that level until growth began again in the 1980s to the current level of approximately 2,600. This mirrors the regeneration of the town, with many new small businesses and innovative community projects which have carried Wiveliscombe buoyantly into the 21st century.

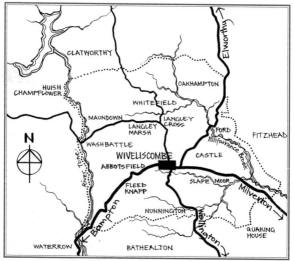

Parish map

Wandering in Wiveliscombe

Walk One

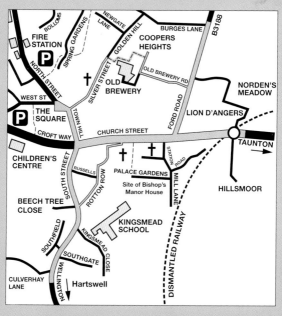

Wiveliscombe South and East
[approx. 3 kilometres]

The Square c.1921

Originally known as the Market Place, the social and commercial centre of Wiveliscombe is **The Square**, although by no means conforming to its geometric name. Believed to have been laid out in the 13th century by order of the Bishop for his economic benefit, and at the top of the hill to protect his privacy, the nucleus of the medieval town had a two-storied thatched market house. On either side of this were the Shambles (butchers' market) and other stalls.

Old Market House

Wiveliscombe.
Cudgel,
OR
Sword and Dagger
Playing,
In the MARKET-PLACE,
On Trinity Tuesday,
BY 4 o'CLOCK,
for
A Purse of Guineas.
Encouragement will be Given to
YOUNG PLAYERS.
DATED THE 28 OF JUNE, 1821.

1821 Poster

The market house was replaced by the **Town Hall** in 1842. Richard Carver (c.1792-1862), who had drawn the plans for the replacement parish church, was employed by Lord Ashburton, the lord of the manor, to design this new building. On 8 September 1841 General Sir George Adams (1779-1856) of Oakhampton Manor laid the foundation stone, in which were sealed some coins and a brass plate. It was opened on 3 August 1842.

1887 Map

It has always been privately owned and, although now known as the Town Hall, it was originally the Assembly Rooms. The upper hall was used for the Magistrates' Court and was also the focus for public events, such as concerts, balls, lantern lectures, silent movies and other social occasions. MPs were presented from the balcony over the now lost portico, and the ground floor area was used for markets.

Ashburton Sale Catalogue 1894

In the 1894 Ashburton sale, as a result of a crisis in the family bank, Baring Brothers, the Town Hall was purchased for £1,100 by John Merchant, a local corn factor, who sold it to the fledgling Co-operative Society just after the 1914-18 War.

WIVELISCOMBE
MUTUAL IMPROVEMENT SOCIETY

Opening stanza of a poetical review written for the
Society's first anniversary meeting
held at the
Town Hall, 8 February 1854

On a Wintry night in 'Fifty-two
Some gentry met, they were but few;
Their object was to make a movement
And form a class for self improvement.
And as they talked of what they'd do,
Some almost sunk with such a view;
Lectures they said should form a part
On History, Sciences, and on Art. ...
And to instruct, and to amuse,
We'll have the town and country news,
And books abundant, too, supply
To tempt the students' eager eye. ...

Town Hall

Continuing clockwise around The Square, the simple
entrance to **No. 10** belies a large, gracious house behind.
From the 1860s, this was the home of the Bond family,
wine and spirit merchants, founded in 1829 by Thomas
Bond. He is buried in the churchyard[1] with his widow
and eight of their eleven children. They were followed by
the Merchant family, corn factors who also had a shop in

North Street. **Whelans café**
in the corner, as with many
other buildings, has housed
various businesses, including
ironmongers, plumbers and a
wine merchant.

*Wiveliscombe Cricket
Club Dinner 1951*

Concert Programme 1894

[1] *Sancti Stones* (Colden Publications, 2001) plot D25.

Once the Bell Inn, **London House**, one of three edifices in The Square that had a fine portico, was so-named by the Thorne Brothers when they moved their drapery and outfitters shop here from Silver Street in the mid 1920s. The business continued under several different names until it closed in 1976. Then the building rapidly deteriorated and was ruinous enough to be used

London House 1970s

as a set for a film about the Troubles in Northern Ireland. The Department of Transport wanted it demolished because of the long traffic queues caused by the narrow West Street but the Department of the Environment stepped in and listed the building. The traffic problem was solved by the construction of Croft Way in 1980.

In 1984, London House was renovated to become shops and flats. In front is the Parish Notice Board, and tourist information marker post created by local artist Michael Fairfax in 2003; one of seven such markers in Taunton Deane.

The White Hart Hotel, once the Green Dragon, was owned by the Hancocks from 1805. A largely unchanged exterior, but it once had a portico, and the current dining room, previously a chemist's shop, was absorbed by the hotel at the end of the 1950s.

It was here on 20 October 1817, after the laying of the foundation stone for the Wellington Monument, that Lord Somerville (1765-1819), the prominent agriculturist from Fitzhead Court, presided over a commemorative dinner. The hotel continues to host local societies, receptions and events. Close to the corner with North Street is one of the series of plaques to be seen around the town, commissioned by the Wiveliscombe Arts Consortium and installed in 2004. They commemorate the town's brewing heritage with a Trail conceived by a local charity, the Jim Laker Fund.

The Square

PUBLIC HOUSES AND INNS IN WIVELISCOMBE

Compiled by Dixon Luxton,
based on Harold Newman Inder's 1948 list

Anchor Inn	4 Church Street
Angel Inn	12 Town Hill
	(later Courtyard)
Bampton Inn (Hotel)	West Road
	(Abbotsfield Cottages site)
Bear Inn	10 North Street
Bell Inn	The Square
	(now London House)
Black Dog	Junction Taunton & Ford Roads
Blue Ball	Church St
	(opposite The Old Cottage)
Borough Inn	15 Golden Hill
Bristol Inn	South of Parrick's Place, South Street
Deepleigh	Langley on Whitefield Road
Five Bells Inn	1 & 2 North Street
Fountain Inn	26 West Street
	(once at 1 Town Hill)
George Inn	14 West Street
	(moved from The Square)
Half Moon Inn	Church Street
	(near church gates)
King's Arms	14 North Street
	(Garden Shop)
Lamb Inn	2 Silver Street
Lion Hotel	2 Town Hill
Mason's Arms	4 Russells
New Inn	25 Golden Hill
Noah's Ark	7 Rotton Row
Royal Oak Inn	18 Church Street
Swan Inn	5 Silver Street
Temperance Hotel	Corner of Town Hill and Croft Way
Three Horseshoes	Langley Marsh
Travellers Rest	Site of Pulsford Lodge
Vintage	10 The Square
White Hart Inn	The Square
	(previously Green Dragon)
White Horse Inn	6 North Street

There are also records of The Bee, The Greyhound and The Sun in the 18th century but locations are not known. An earlier document of 1656 refers to The Beare, The George, The Angell, The Lion, The Lamb and The Bell, of which only the Bear survives. Although called inns, many were normal domestic houses from which beer brewed on the premises was sold.

Although a **pharmacy** since 1985, for nearly one hundred years this building, with Egyptian embellishments on the

C C Richard's Emporium

roof, served the needs of farmers when they came in for the monthly market. From the early 1880s, it belonged to William Langdon, 'saddle, collar and harness maker; every article in the trade executed in the best style'. Thomas, his son, moved the business to Berrys on Town Hill in 1906. A member

of the West Street family, Clifford Cyril Richards then established a hardware store in the property which continued for twenty years by others after his death in 1965. C C Richards sold everything from sofas, soap powder, spades and spanners to saucepans and soup spoons and his emporium stretched out at the back to the cattle market behind.

Roof top embellishment

Court House

Court House

The Community Office, which opened in May 2002, was previously Lloyds Bank, the successor in business to the Hancock's bank. **Court House** was built by William Hancock (1810-96) in 1881 for his family of eleven children. The house had four reception rooms, a billiard room, a grand central staircase and seventeen bedrooms, but only one bathroom. The external timber decoration, including dates and initials, is contemporary. Interior panelling came from properties acquired by the family during the expansion of the brewing business. Following the death in 1909 of Mary, his widow, Court House was sold to E J Thorne, a local

entrepreneur, undertaker and pillar of the Congregational Church, who moved his house furnishing business (est. 1750) from West Street. Interestingly, many aspects of that business are mirrored today in the current occupant, Courthouse Interiors. During the 1939-45 War the building housed a 'British Restaurant',

Drawn by Sir Alfred Munnings

one of a national chain of community-run kitchens with controlled prices. At the same time, a substantial part of this once gracious home was converted into flats, accessed from the alleyway to the east of the pharmacy. This alley also leads to **Castle Cottage**, with its distinctive mitre-shaped gable.

THE MARRIAGE OF WILLIAM AND MARY HANCOCK'S ONLY DAUGHTER LUCY WITH STEPHEN G WILLIAMS ON 29 MAY 1890

God Bless Ye Wedded Pair

GAY WEDDING AT WIVELISCOMBE ... a very handsome triumphal arch, representing an old baronial castle, was erected by the employees of Mr Hancock. Its embattled ivy-clad walls were a capital representation and exceedingly artistic. Round the archway facing the Bank appeared the words 'May their lives go cheerily'... and on the other side 'God Bless Ye Wedded Pair'. [*West Somerset Free Press*, Saturday 31 May 1890]

The bride was given a horse called *Ten to One* by her ten brothers, and a red carpet was laid from Court House all the way to St Andrew's. Flags flew from the church tower and bunting was strung around the town. This day was regarded as a general holiday.

The eastern side of the Court House with the arched doorway was the offices of the Wiveliscombe Bank, which had been founded by the Hancocks in 1803 and was a branch of the National Provincial Bank from the 1920s. The strong-rooms remain in the basement of both this ex-bank building and the Community Office. From 1972, the Library was housed in the old Bank office, until its move across The Square in 2010.

1884 Bank note

Stuckey's Bank, now part of NatWest

Webbers Estate Agents' office was previously Doble & Prout, gentlemen's tailors and outfitters. Mr Prout used to sit sewing at a window above the shop looking down Town Hill. Across the narrow entrance to Silver Street, where there is now a gift shop, was another gents' outfitter, John Cox. In the 1940s, part of what had been Mr Cox's shop was briefly used by the Roman Catholic community as a church, when the influx of evacuees and displaced persons swelled the congregation.

Tailor's and Outfitters

Tailor's Label

The **Newsagents**, once a high-quality stationer, printer and bookseller, was founded by John Vickery (1834-1913) in 1854. In the 18th century it had been The Fountain Inn, where local worthies of the Wiveliscombe Club met and the seeds of the idea of a school and dispensary were germinated.

Mrs Octavia Parsons (1869-1962), one of John Vickery's twenty-three children, ran the family firm until her death. She was always immaculately dressed, and knew everything that was going

Vickery
Sewing Box

on, keeping an eye on proceedings and offering wise counsel from her hideaway at the back of the shop.

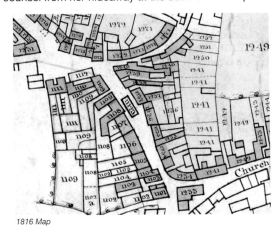

1816 Map

Until the 1939-45 War, the small triangular hairdressers on the corner of Town Hill and The Square also sold confectionery, sweets and tobacco. Charlie Chidgey, the proprietor, is remembered for his 'very waxed moustache'.

Town Hill

TOWN HILL (also known as High Street but originally Fore Street) was an area of commercial enterprise including three drapers and outfitters and three hotels. Buildings shown in the map halfway down the hill and again at Cheapside had been demolished by the time of the Richard Beadon sale in 1834.

On the right at the top is the **The Lion Hotel**, once the premier hotel in the town, and owned by the Hancocks. The mail coach called here en route between Taunton and Barnstaple from 1827. Social functions, such as Friendly Society meetings and the Fatstock and Dispensary Trust dinners, were held here. After the closure of the hotel, it was sold to the Christian Fellowship in 1955. They amalgamated with the Congregational Church in 1979. The building and its stabling, laundry and bowling alley have been converted into offices, flats

Lion Hotel

and cottages. A lion has recently been placed over the arched entrance to the courtyard to replace the original which disappeared overnight in 1955.

Uppingtons, the substantial red-brick house at No. 6, was built by a family of that name in 1693. Anne Uppington married James Lean (1704-68), who came from Ireland with his brother and settled in Wiveliscombe in 1737. The house was occupied until 1915 by the Leans, a prominent non-conformist family.

Uppingtons

ROBERT HAWKINS	W. C. & E. M. BAIGENT	DOBLE & PROUT	H. G. & L. M. BROWNSEY
Family Butcher	DRAPERS and COSTUMIERS	SOMERSET HOUSE WIVELISCOMBE	*Jewellers* High St., WIVELISCOMBE
HIGH STREET WIVELISCOMBE	*Ladies' and Children's Wear* WIVELISCOMBE *Phone 251*	TAILORS & OUTFITTERS HOSIERS & HATTERS — BOOT, SHOE and LEGGING WAREHOUSE *Phone 360*	INGERSOLL WATCHES SMITH'S CLOCKS FANCY JEWELLERY — BIRO PENS —

The **Golden Ocean** Chinese takeaway was for many years a pharmacy, conveniently opposite the Dispensary.

James Osborne, the proprietor from 1902-1927, was also a photographer. As with other shops on the hill, Milners (later Baigent's) became a restaurant and cake shop, then an estate agents and is now **St Margaret's Hospice** shop, reflecting how businesses have come and gone but the buildings have remained relatively unchanged.

Osborne's Pharmacy

No.12, The Courtyard Inn until 2010, was once Mrs Jell's Guesthouse, and previously the Angel Hotel, another coaching inn. The Revenue Office was located behind, where the excise duties were paid. There are local legends of tunnels along which the beer barrels were rolled from the brewery to the inns, thus avoiding the taxman. Certainly, over the years, holes have opened up in the roads around the town, but these could be merely old water or drainage channels.

Collard's shop   *Brownsey's shop*

Aisle Altar Hymn (No. 14). Watches and clocks had been made or repaired in the town from at least 1700 until 2003, when Michael Wren ceased trading. Herbert G Brownsey, whose jewellery business began in 1926, also occupied these premises, which at an earlier stage had been a shoe shop, Collard's Stores, until their move across the road.

The warehouse of Small's, corn, feed and coal merchants, was located where there is now a private **parking area** next to the traffic lights. In the old granary buildings behind were Lee & Beilen, run by a London evacuee family who made timing mechanisms

Pearse Clock c.1880

and specialised parts for military equipment during the 1939-45 War. Their change to making electric clocks (as Timlec Ltd) in 1946 did not prosper; the business closed and the family emigrated to California.

Temperance Hotel

Temperance Hotel in the 1930's

At the **traffic lights**, then a T-junction, the Temperance Hotel faced down Church Street. In the 1889 *Kelly's Directory*, Charles Bull, the proprietor, optimistically described this family and commercial hotel as being only two minutes walk from the railway station. A few years later he was succeeded by Fred Parkman. In the early 1920s it became Hall's Restaurant, continuing to provide accommodation. Later, the restaurant became a fish and chip shop. In the 1970s the near-derelict building was demolished. Croft Way was built in 1980.

Back again to the top of Town Hill, on the left (east) next to the newsagents, the archway leads to **Printers Mews**, the site of Mr Vickery's print-shop. The short-lived *Wiveliscombe Miscellany & General Advertiser* (1854), and the *Wiveliscombe Express* (1896-1928) are both believed to have been printed here.

Wiveliscombe Express 1898

The house, **Cranmers**, recalls the apothecary Mr Bishop Cranmer, who founded the Dispensary with his nephew, the surgeon, Dr Henry Sully. The attractive residence, No. 5, **Berrys**, appropriately named Verandah House in the late 19th century, became the family home of the legendary Mrs Bessie Langdon, who we will meet again in Church Street (see page 23). Tommy Langdon moved his saddlers' business here from The Square in 1906 at the time of his marriage to Bessie. A 12th century font, found in the garden in the 1920s, was installed in St Andrew's church.

The bold date, '**1804**', over the door of The Dispensary commemorates the year when a forerunner to the National Health Service (NHS) was set up for the people of the district in The Fountain (now the newsagents at the top of the hill).

Dispensary Entrance

In 1839 this building was called Mitchells. William Hancock, one of the prime movers in the establishment of The Dispensary, sold the property to the Management Committee, which met monthly until the formation of the NHS in 1948. Surgeries continued here, except for a period in the 1950s, until the Lister House surgery opened in 1986 in Bollams Mead.

One of the founders, Bishop Cranmer (1748-1831), a direct descendant of Archbishop Cranmer, was trained in London. Simple and unostentatious in diet and dress, Cranmer, in the manner of the time, hunted with his own hounds twice a week for over fifty years. He was buried in St Andrew's churchyard.

The other was Cranmer's nephew, Henry Sully (1770-1847), who married a local girl Maria Waldron in 1793 and the following year moved to Wiveliscombe. Sully specialised in the treatment of cancer and eye diseases. Although appointed a court physician (he treated the eyes of the 5th son of King George III, the Duke of Cumberland), he spent much of his time here. Initially Dr Sully covered the Dispensary expenses himself but, from 1816, subscribers and donors from near and far provided the funds. Dr Sully retired in 1832 and moved to Okehills, near Taunton, but he was buried at Wiveliscombe.

Another business occupying part of Mitchells is the **Carousel Pig**, an innovative gift and clothing shop.

Wilkie, May & Tuckwood Estate Agents have occupied this double-fronted building since 1994, replacing a hairdressing business. In the 1834 Richard Beadon sale, it was called Bennisons and was occupied by members of the Hancock family. It was later Collard's Stores selling boots and shoes after their move from across the street before the 1939-45 War.

The narrow **Lamb Lane**, just to the south of Wilkies, is a reminder of the town's early and long involvement with the woollen industry. A row of houses at right angles to the street, such as these, is a typical feature of old towns. In the 17th

Collards boot department

and 18th centuries, although important, wool was only a cottage industry with many small-scale artisans working on various stages of production in their houses or outbuildings. Clothiers, or mercers, who often financed the workers with loans, bought the finished cloth. Such clothiers issued token coins in the 17th and 19th centuries which were used as currency locally. The Hancocks had been involved in the wool trade in neighbouring parishes until moving to Wiveliscombe.

Lawyers **Risdon Hosegood**, at No.17, are successors to the solicitor Thomas Vincent Pearse (1862-1947) whose brother left money for the recreation ground and pavilion.

Featherstone Trade Token 1814

No.19 was the shop of Robert 'Bobbie' Hawkins (1870-1956), the

Jim & Don Webber

butcher. He set up his business c.1894, and upon his death it passed to his two young nephews, brothers Don and Jim Webber, who had worked there since leaving school aged 14. Their shop had a pair of enormous cattle horns on the wall and a huge, solid chopping block made from a whole tree trunk. When Don and Jim retired in 1993, the shop closed after serving the community for about 100 years. Bobbie's brother Frederick Joseph Hawkins (1877-1936)

was also a butcher, with a shop first in North Street, later in West Street. In the first half of the 20th century each butcher had his own slaughter facilities and they also produced their own sausages, bacon, brawn and pies.

Town Hill Butcher est. 1894

Cheapside, on the corner by the traffic lights, indicates that this was once also a market area (in medieval English *cheap* means market). As with Hawkins the butchers, several other small shops have now become private houses, including **No. 23**, Mrs Langford's sweet shop, and next door, Miss Tuckfield's small greengrocery.

Cheapside

Gullet looking south

South Street was previously known as Gullet, a name recalling the drain which carried water from the higher parts of the town down to the Lamb Brook. When Croft Way was constructed, the sunken pathway in front of the Temperance Hotel down into South Street disappeared. The surface of the small courtyard on your right demonstrates the level of the old footpath.

Vicarage built 1846

The **Old Vicarage** dates from 1846, and the current **Rectory** was built in its extensive grounds in 1966. Wiveliscombe suffered from the curious three-tier system of clergy common in the 19th century. The Rector had a freehold interest in land within the parish but was often an absentee landlord. He would appoint a Vicar to look after the parish, but even he was able to delegate to a curate. Prior to 1846, the clergy lived in the church compound.

Reverend Howard McCririck

Opposite is **The Cottage** with its 'Gothic' style windows, home for over thirty years of Marian (1863-1958), widow of Reverend Howard McCririck (1859-1922), the well-respected vicar for thirty-one years. He built chapels in the neighbourhood at Langley Marsh and Croford and there was no society or club in the town he did not support or in which he was not an active and genial participant. Previously The Cottage had been the home of Mrs Mainwaring whose husband, Horatio (son of an Admiral) was in the Indian Woods and Forestry Service, and is buried in the churchyard.

The Cottage 1872

Wesleyan Chapel

One of three smithies marked on an 1887 map of the town stood at the corner of Russells. The bold fronted **chapel** of the Wesleyan Methodists dates from 1845. Wesleyanism, which had come to the town in 1791, had thrived and outgrown its smaller chapel on Golden Hill. Seating 250, this chapel was built by Teddy Nurcombe for £364. In 1920 a new organ was installed, and the basement school room was used as a medical centre by the US Army during the 1939-45 War. With the decline in churchgoing, services ceased in June 1986. Since being sold, the building has been used for both residential and commercial purposes.

Wesleyan Chapel 1986

Pottery remains of early medieval date indicate long occupation of this part of the town. Post-medieval tanyards, upstream of the Bishop's Manor, suggest this noxious trade flourished after the latter became derelict. The trade is recalled by a field named Tanners, reached by the footpath heading west opposite Russells. Cottages, built for the tanyard workers in this area, were enlarged in the mid-19th century. The Hayes, once a dame school, was built c.1845

Parricks Place

and named after its builder. Across the road is Parricks Place, once a row of nine cottages. The name recalls a family known to have been in the area in the 18th century. At the south end of the row was the Bristol Inn.

Beech Tree Close recalls the tree, cut down in 1985, that grew in the grounds of the once-gracious Lambrook House. The house, named after a stream which now passes under the site via a culvert, was built c.1815 by

Lambrook House

tanner, William Webber, who was related by marriage to the Hancocks. Among other owners were the long established leading town families, the Bouchers and Lutleys, and Willoughby Hancock who lived there for twenty years before moving to Abbotsfield in 1933. During the 1939-45 War, the house was used by American servicemen who had a vehicle park

The beech tree, axed 1985

across the road on Lambrook Meadow. Post-war, Smalls, the corn and coal merchants, moved down from Town Hill. After the house was demolished in the 1960s, Western National used the site for parking buses.

In 1835 the National School, under the chairmanship of the Vicar, Revd John Sunderland, was established in the tall building on the right, known locally as the **Church School**. Constructed on the site of cottages, it benefits from windows and a stone lozenge believed to have been removed from the derelict Bishop's manor.

The buildings have been converted into a residence and workshop. In the wall is a water supply point, details of which may be found in WALK TWO, page 38.

Mid-19th century engraving

Sancti Plot

Opposite the school are **Drain Steps**, an old passage way leading up to **Church Street**. The houses on the south of the street (westwards towards the traffic lights) are some of the oldest of the town, many in the past having contained small businesses. **No.14** was the home of photographer and shoe-shop proprietor Mr George Wm French, who had a family of five boys and seven girls. He had a dormer window installed in the roof to give better light to his studio.

Many of his portraits and postcard views survive. After his death in 1929, his daughter Hildred continued with the shoe-shop. Other businesses on the south side of the street were another photographer,

Hildred French

Lempriere, a bicycle shop, a barber, a tailor, a grocer and three inns: the Anchor, Royal Oak and Half Moon. Public houses organised outings for their customers, or other groups within the town such as the bell-ringers.

Royal Oak outing

Church Street

Albert Place
looking north

Near the traffic lights were the offices of Risdon's, then auctioneers, and Moger & Couch, solicitors. On the north side is **Queen's Terrace**, with its steep back gardens, and the double-fronted house, at **No. 11** was the Congregational Church manse from 1850 until 1945. No.15, **Churchview Cottage**, was a pair of one-up, one-down cottages with an archway leading to Albert Place. This row of six little cottages was approached by a cobbled alley and stood at right angles to the main road. Known affectionately as Puddlecourt, or Tramps Alley, the houses were condemned in the late 1950s and demolished.

Entrance to Albert Place 1953

The **fish and chip shop** occupies the premises of one of the several bakers in the town. Barringtons was founded nearly one hundred years ago and closed in 1961. Not only did they bake bread, cakes, meat and fruit pies, shortbread etc, but they also had tables where teas were served. To the east of this, where a driveway leads up to modern bungalows, there were three more tiny cottages facing Church Street, behind which had been a thatched barn and stables, all demolished in the late 1960s.

Half Moon, Church Street

Barrington's Bakery

The house called **Braynes**, now split into two, was built c.1650 by a prominent member of the Society of Friends, the apothecary Francis Brayne. In the garden a cobbled avenue lined with box trees, known as the 'Monks Walk', is believed to be an ancient route from the Bishop's manor to Golden Hill. There is also a gazebo where Captain Frederick Marryat (the children's author) is reputed to have

Captain Marryat 1792-1844

written *Mr Midshipman Easy* in 1836. In 1866, his daughter Caroline Cecilia married Dr George Robert

Catherine Marryat's gravestone

Norris, the town medical officer from 1866-1903 and they lived at Braynes. Catherine, Marryat's widow, died in 1883 and is buried in the churchyard.

Braynes is one of a number of large houses hereabouts remodelled by Clarence 'Gassy' Harris (1887-1980). He was with the Taunton Gas Light & Coke Company for twenty-nine years and, after retiring as Managing Director in 1945, devoted his time to property development, including Abbotsfield and Oakhampton Manor.

Crossing the road, the garden plot on your right as you approach the church gates contained the Half Moon Inn and the Bellew family home.

The old church from the south

Parish Church of St Andrew

The churchyard, which serves all denominations, is one of the largest in Somerset still open for burials. In 1829, when the church was rebuilt, the graveyard was enlarged by demolishing a row of cottages between the church and Church Street and the ground level was raised, thereby obscuring evidence of older burials. Full details of those recorded in the church or buried in the churchyard, including a Waterloo veteran, John Bale who died in 1861, may be found in *Sancti Stones* (Colden Publications, 2001). This includes all those commemorated on the

St Andrew's

two war memorials outside the north door. Further war memorials are located on the Recreation Ground (see WALK TWO).

Tradition has it that the churchyard should be walked around clockwise to avoid upsetting the spirits. There are several yew trees, including a young one presented by the Diocese for the Millennium.

The **cross** to the north of the church is one of the earliest surviving structures in the town. Believed to date from the fourteenth century, it is possibly linked to Bishop Drokensford (1309-29) who built the nearby Manor House. From the east end of the church, you can see the medieval gatehouse to this Manor House. A row of houses, Palace Gardens, was built on this site by William White

Ancient Cross

1914-18 War Memorial

in the 1930s to occupy his employees during the recession. Excavation in the area has revealed traces of walls and medieval pottery and tile fragments dating from the 14th or 15th centuries.

Although a church in this parish was first documented in 1179, it is known that Bishop Ralph (1329-63) built a church here which, in 1791, Collinson recorded as having a 'beautiful carved oak screen, huge square pews' and a number of galleries for private use. Not long afterwards it was found to be unsafe: the pillars were out of perpendicular, and the tower rocked when the bells were rung. Repairs would have cost £3,100, but it was decided to rebuild for £4,200. In spite of the major structural problems, when the church was taken down in 1827 gunpowder was required to demolish the old tower. One major change was the move of the entrance from the south to the north side. The designer was Richard Carver, the County Surveyor, who was also responsible for the Town Hall and other church and secular projects in Somerset. The box pews were part of his unique design to seat 1,250 worshippers; the churchwardens were paid rent for pews with doors, whilst any without were 'free and unappropriated for ever'. Those in the north and south aisles have been removed.

Ivory gavel

Church door bosses

The inscribed ivory gavel used in the ceremony to lay the foundation stone on 6 June 1827 was provided by the local Masonic Lodge, and records the names of most of the worthies of the town at the time. The new St Andrew's was consecrated by the Bishop, George Henry Law, on 27 October 1829.

The rose window was inserted in 1915. It was designed by Miss Alice Erskine as a memorial to Lt Ralph Escott Hancock DSO, son of Phillip and Mariquita Hancock, who had been killed in action at Festubert on 29 October 1914. It displaced the portrait of Christ by William Brockedon (1787-1854) which was presented to the church by his patron General Sir George Adams, of

19th Century Interior

Oakhampton, and now hangs in the north aisle. There are a number of memorial tablets to others who gave their lives in both World Wars, and a large wooden panel listing those who served.

In the South Aisle is the Wyndham monument, commemorating Humphrey and Margery Windham [sic]. In the 17th century, their only daughter Elizabeth Colles founded almshouses at Abbotsfield and the name lives on in the Wyndham Flats built on the site of their family home on Golden Hill. The organ, of which Wiveliscombe is justifiably proud, dates from 1829 and has been upgraded over the years, most recently in 2000. There are eight bells in the tower, four of which are dated 1751. They were re-cast, re-hung and re-dedicated in 1965.

Looking north over Braynes

Sancti Stones records the interments in the thirty-six catacombs under the re-built church, the last of which took place in 1926. A plaque in the south aisle records how the empty vaults were used during 1939-45 War as a safe storage place for a considerable quantity of stained glass, silver, documents and irreplaceable furnishings from churches, synagogues and museums in London and elsewhere. Recently, part of the crypt has been converted into a meeting room.

Returning to Church Street, turn right and shortly you will pass the **Old Cottage**, once three dwellings called Cat's Cottages and converted in 1920 by Major A F Davey, Secretary to the Somerset County Cricket Club 1923-31. The whole area to the east of the churchyard was the Palace Green, with a mid-15th century barn, which was used for services whilst the new St Andrew's was being built. Here local fairs and festivities took place, such as cock fighting, bull baiting and cudgel playing.

Opposite is **Caradoc**. This unusual name was given by previous owners to remember their courtship in the hills of Shropshire.

Church Street c. 1950

Bournes, the oldest residence of substance in the town, was largely built by Gilbert Bourne, Bishop of Bath & Wells (1554-60). He was deprived of his see and expelled by Queen Elizabeth I because he was appointed during the reign of Queen Mary (1553-58), and remained true to his Catholic faith after her death. He was

Fair Poster 1832

confined in the Tower of London for three years, and died in 1569 at Silverton, Devon, still a prisoner of the church authorities.

Westbourne   St Richard's church

The **Roman Catholic Church** was designed by Bristol architects Ivor, Day & O'Brien, and built by Pearce & Sons. It is dedicated to St Richard of Chichester and was consecrated by Bishop Rudderham of Clifton in 1967. The church stands on the site of Mrs Langdon's egg-packing factory.

In the 1930s Mrs Bessie Langdon (née Hill) (1881-1959) moved to **Westbourne House**, which subsequently has been both the presbytery for St Richard's and a veterinary practice. From humble beginnings selling eggs from her parents' farm, Mrs Langdon's business grew to the extent that in September 1939 she employed twenty-five people and supplied two tons of eggs, a thousand chickens, and two thousand rabbits each week to the London market. After the war, the business expanded into transport and in 1956 she retired and handed over the flourishing enterprise to her two sons. She died three years later and is buried in Wiveliscombe.

Mason's Panel

A panel in the Dining Room of the White Hart, Wiveliscombe, which was the Lodge Room of the first Loyal Vacation Lodge.

Original panel in White Hart

Next door, the second of the two handsome buildings built by the Hancocks for their senior office staff, is **Eastbourne House**. The Masonic Loyal Vacation Lodge, No. 67, was founded in 1802 by the leading citizens of the town and met at the White Hart. The Lodge was revived in 1946 and moved to this building in 1960, bringing with them the original meeting room panel.

Turning into Station Road, the **Bishops Green** houses on the right were built in the 1990s on the site of Goodland's builders merchant and coal yard. Station Road remains on the same alignment as the 1816 map. The **Railway Station** opened in June 1871 at the then end of the line from Taunton; in November 1873, the route was completed through to Barnstaple. The line was built to Brunel's 'broad' gauge of 7ft ¼in, and was converted to

Station pre-1881

Station c. 1900

'standard' gauge, 4ft 8½in, in 1881. In 1876, mail was first carried on the line. Many other opportunities were opened up including carrying stock to and from the cattle market; taking horses to Exmoor for hunting; going to Taunton for school or Saturday night cinema; and in

View over Ashbeers

wartime there were trains full of rabbits for the London markets. The last passenger train ran on 3 October 1966 (freight having ceased in 1964); subsequently the station buildings, most of which survive intact, and the surrounding yards have become useful industrial sites. A working model of the station and the area is regularly exhibited at the annual Horticultural Society show at Kingsmead.

Southwest of the railway station is the site of the bishop's manor complex. Little is known of the layout of the domestic buildings but, by 1841, few buildings were still standing, except for a cluster in the northwest corner that included the 17th century Poor House. **Town Mill** is mentioned in Domesday; some fragments survive despite modern development, and the archaeological potential of the area remains high. The mill pond was probably kept stocked with fish for the Bishop. Although now filled in, it survived at least until 1916 when it froze over enabling people to skate.

In the southeast corner of the junction of Station Road and Taunton Road stood a two-storey house often referred to as 'The Tollhouse'. 19th century maps and plans confirm that the tollhouse and gate were on the north side of the Taunton road, part of **April Cottage**.

April Cottage

Taunton Road 1902

From this point, there is the opportunity to curtail this Walk, by returning to The Square along Church Street and up Town Hill.

The truncated embankment at the roundabout is the only remaining trace of where the railway crossed the road by a bridge. The **Norden's Meadow** houses were built by Westbury Homes between 1996-98 and a number suffered from a disastrous flood when a violent storm

fell on Maundown and the town on 13 May 1998. *Wifela's Combe* gives an interesting account of another great storm which did an immense amount of damage in the parish in May 1811. To the south is the slaughterhouse, built in 1990, with the Hillsmoor sewage farm beyond, where previously there were withy beds.

Three distinctive carved and painted **markers** illustrating aspects of the town were

Marker Posts

designed and made by Robert Koenig and erected in 2003. The **town name** sign was installed in May 2005 as part of the celebrations of twenty years of twinning arrangements with Le Lion d'Angers in France.

Moving into **Ford Road**, previously called Frog Lane (frogs are still found in the Lion d'Angers estate),

Clerkspool, on the left, was once a farm house. Long since demolished were a number of farm cottages on the site of No. 5 Ford Road, where Harry Nation built the present house in 1921. Opposite, the **Toll Gate** development of 2004 is on the site of Greedy's sawmills, undertakers, builders

and wood yard. The builders' yard was taken over by Jim Pincombe, before being bought by Rawle Gammon and Baker Ltd (RGB), who have now moved to premises on Old Brewery Road.

Greedy's Yard with Treligga beyond

Mayfield Terrace was built by Mr W Endicott 'as a speculation'. The unfinished north end and off-centre name plaque confirm its incomplete status. The decorative iron railings were removed by the Council during the 1939-45 War.

Mayfield Terrace

The recently renovated red-brick bungalow opposite was one of two in the town built by Cornishmen. **Treligga** was built c.1935 by the owner of Manor Garage, Robert 'Bobby' Sweet, who bequeathed it to the Congregational Church and it became their manse in 1945. Three houses were constructed in the garden after Treligga had been sold a few years ago. The other 'Cornish' dwelling situated further north up Ford Road, **Trelawny**, was built in 1941 by Harold Screech, railway signalman. It is believed this was the only house in Wiveliscombe to have taken German fire during the 1939-45 War, although others on Golden Hill took tracer bullets when the brewery tower caught German attention.

In 1960, Taunton Vale Industries (TVI), designers and makers of chopping boards, trays, and co-ordinated kitchen items, moved into purpose-built premises now occupied by EPS Ltd. The red-brick factory next on the left has been variously a Langdon egg-packing station, a road transport depot, Maynards Bakery, Whites the

TVI Key rack

Puttees

builders, and is now the offices of the Cotleigh Brewery. Foremost Furniture occupies the Fox Brothers' 1902 weaving shed, where grey pinstripe suiting and puttees were manufactured, continuing the town's long links with the woollen industry.

'WIVELISCOMBE IN 1806'
by Thomas Newton

But the trade of the place was in woollen goods – blanketings, grey cloth, and blue cloth called Pennystones. The latter was made in great abundance. Nearly all the work was done by hand – there was very little machinery – spinning, warping, weaving, cleansing, dying, tentering, napping etc. [*Somerset County Gazette*, 17 May 1856]

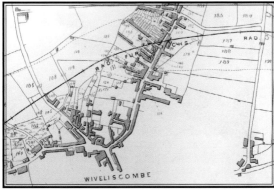
Proposed railway alignment 1864

The estate to the east was built by Tarmac in 1989-90, and was named to honour the French town of **Le Lion d'Angers** with which Wiveliscombe has had a twinning relationship since 1985. Part of this site was named Butts Close in the 1834 Beadon sale, suggesting a medieval site for archery practice.

Victorian letterbox

Prospect House (now **Tor House**), at the junction of Ford Road and Burges Lane, is said to have been built as the Station Hotel. The plan misfired when the line was built further south. Behind Tor House was the parish pound, and in the wall is an 1860s letterbox. There are two other Victorian boxes in the parish still with a daily collection.

Wellington Terrace, in Burges Lane, was built for Fox's employees when that Wellington firm opened here in 1902. The 19th century field name is recalled in **Durhams Cottages**, of similar date, built for Hancock's brewery workers.

Tor House

Wellington Terrace

Durhams Cottages

View south from Prospect

The route now takes you back to **Old Brewery Road** which crosses 'The Piggins', once an area of allotment gardens and pig pens. The **Drill Hall** was built in the mid-1930s and during the 1939-45 War was used as a cookhouse by the Americans. The nearby **Scout Hut** was opened in 1979 by local resident, the late The Hon. Mrs Betty Clay, CBE (1917-2004) daughter of Lord Baden-Powell, on the site of a previous hut erected in the 1930s. Other industrial buildings along this road are more recent and house a number of small specialised businesses including Yaffle Engineering, Gemberry and WCI Pollution Control.

At the end of Old Brewery Road there is a pedestrian right-of-way up to Golden Hill. Just beyond RGB, it turns right towards Coopers Heights, then up the steep concrete roadway on the left, passing Exmoor Ales and Quantock Engineering, to emerge onto Golden Hill. Turn left and the Walk returns to The Square. A less steep return to The Square is to retrace your footsteps to the traffic lights, and up Town Hill.

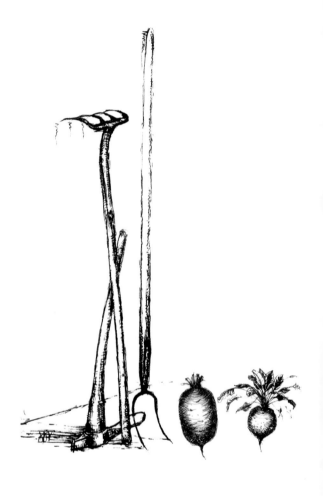

Wandering in Wiveliscombe

Walk Two

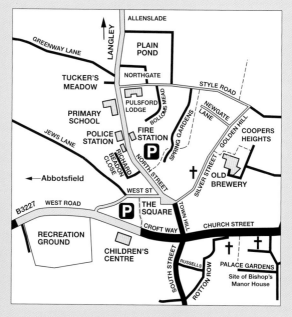

Wiveliscombe North and West
[approx. 2.7 kilometres]

From the Square we enter **Silver Street**, previously a much more active commercial area. On opposite sides, at the entrance to the street, were two tailors and outfitters, Doble & Prout, now an estate agents, and J C Cox, on the right, now part of the newsagent's premises. Next on the right was the Lamb Inn, now named Old Inn, opposite which was the **Swan**. **Wivey Washer** (the Laundrette) was previously Hewlett's, a pork butcher. Behind this

shop and the Newsagent is a disused well sunk by the Urban District Council in the 1880s to supplement the town's supply.

William Hole's wireless and cycle shop moved from Church Street in 1935 to **Tower View**, which is now a private residence. After the 1939-45 War, both his sons went into separate garage businesses. Opposite Tower View a private drive leads down to another

Hancock house, **Oak Court**. Replacing older cottages, this 19th century house was used as a convalescent home during the 1914-18 War, and was split into two in the late 1940s. With its attractive locally quarried slate-clad west-facing elevation, it has recently become a single house again.

Oak Court, 1916

The Reading Rooms, No.10, were built to mark Queen Victoria's Golden Jubilee in 1887. Designed by Mr T W F Newton and built by Mr F Richards, they were opened on 10 December 1888. There were two reading rooms, with a billiard room and 'snug' above. The upper floor was used for meetings of The Wiveliscombe Urban District Council until 1933, when it was merged into the Wellington Rural District Council. Between 1946 and 1972 the building housed the public library. It is now a private residence.

Reading Rooms

For a short distance the road widens, and the next buildings on the left side are proportionally much larger. These replace sixteen houses destroyed by a serious fire in April 1863, which had started in a candle factory (est. 1846) run by Thomas Thorne. His replacement premises were the double-fronted building 'London House' which, by 1889, had become Thorne Brothers, *drapers, silk mercers, tailors, hatters and outfitters; grocers, tea dealers and provision merchants; family mourning; funerals furnished.*

When Thornes' moved to what had been the Bell Inn in The Square in the mid 1920s, they took the name 'London House' with them. The shop they vacated became the grocers, Ellerton's Stores. Today, the building houses two studio businesses with residential accommodation above.

No. 16 on the right was the boot and shoe repairer Harold Margetts, grandfather of the late celebrity chef Keith Floyd (1943-2009). The street narrows again before the **Congregational Church** which was built as a chapel for the Independents in 1708. It was enlarged in 1825 and the interior is very handsome. A few years ago a new manse

Original paper bag

was built, and a range of ancillary buildings developed, obscuring some of the small burial ground in use since 1812. The land for this was donated by the Lean family, who also presented an organ, which had once been loaned to Napoleon Bonaparte, and was sold in 1900 to a church in Australia.

Exposed graves in Congregational churchyard   *18th Century Organ*

Opposite, at No. 28 **Vale View**, a leather wallet was found containing the papers of a local man, Jonathan Gore Tudball, a medical student at Guys Hospital in London from 1813, who later worked at the Dispensary on Town Hill. In the 1920s the house became a cyclists' hostel and, in 1934, accommodation was offered through The Cyclists' Touring Club Handbook. No. 26 was part of this same property and in 1875 was a bakery.

In March 1902 a **Liberal Club** was established in the old Friends' Meeting Rooms at Nos. 32 and 34, opposite the Congregational Church car park. A group of volunteers, with professional help, built a skittle alley in 1906.

A substantial house is **Spring Hill**, at No. 40, built circa 1800. During the 1939-45 War, Willoughby Hancock lived here while his home, Abbotsfield, was used as a convalescent home for injured servicemen. On passing Spring Hill, the name of the road changes from Silver Street to Golden Hill. Prior to 1887 the whole length from The Square to the foot of the hill was known variously as Golden Street (or Hill).

Hancock family c. 1880

HANCOCK'S BREWERY AND CIDER FACTORY

William Hancock began brewing in 1805 on Town Hill. Two years later he purchased land and cottages from John Collard for the family business. Because of the run-down of the woollen industry, this was timely as the brewery was to have a considerable impact on the employment opportunities and economy of the town until production ceased in 1959. (For further details, see Mary Miles's *Hancock's Brewery, Wiveliscombe*). The Mews led to the main entrance of the brewery, locally known as 'The Bewrey', much of which has since been demolished. While the Tower, Malthouse and Oast House have been converted to residential use, other buildings house light commercial ventures, including Exmoor Ales, one of two real-ale breweries in the town, the other being Cotleigh on Ford Road. Other areas await redevelopment, which will obliterate the complex underground history of tunnels, chambers, cellars, conduits and water pipes.

Brewery cellar arch 1848

Brewery Chimney

On the western side of the hill, the Wyndham flats stand on the site of the Wyndham family's 17th century town house, which was replaced by Hancock's wine store in 1813. After use as a second malt-house, it was converted in 1917 to become a cider and soft drinks production facility. The upper floor was used for social events and, during the 1939-45 War, as billets.

Hancock employees sampling the brew

Cider factory fire

Brewery receipt

After the company was taken over and all production ceased, these buildings became a warehouse, which was destroyed by a spectacular fire in 1969.

At the **Bell House**, No.1 Golden Hill, a bell was rung for the start of work at the brewery or in case of fire. The position of the bell-cote (now lost) can be seen above the gable end. In 1905 the bell was replaced by a siren (nicknamed 'Willoughby's Wail' after the firm's Chairman) located on the brewery tower. This became the town's fire watch-point during wartime.

Up to forty horses were stabled on Golden Hill. The drays carried barrels and crates up to 25 miles away, and the coming of the railway in 1871 provided opportunities for sales in a wider area. Steam wagons were used from 1904 and later petrol lorries, but horse-drawn local deliveries continued until 1958.

Coronation Lunch ticket, 1937

Brewery Dray

Golden Hill

Mrs Broom's Shop

GOLDEN HILL The name is a puzzle, but a 1522 deed refers to the street as 'Golderney Hill' and a 1708 document calls it 'Golden-Hill-Street'. There are many houses here now, some with wide window lintels indicating previous use as a shop, but in the past the density of population was much greater, with many 'long' families living in quite small dwellings. The narrow garden strips behind, often in multiples of 16½ feet (one rod, pole or perch) wide, reflect their history as burgage plots, dating

Golden Hill Artwork

from the 14th century. Under this ancient form of land tenure, the occupier paid an annual rent to the church, as landowner, to support the poor of the parish. No 'listed' structures of known pre-1700 origin survive in the area.

1864 plan showing burgage plots

No. 15, **Borough House**, is closely linked to the early administration of the town as the Court Leet met here. From early in the 19th century it was the Borough Inn, although beforehand it is believed to have been the Cat & Fiddle. It is interesting to note that a cat and fiddle are carved on the misericord of the Wiveliscombe Prebendal Stall in Wells Cathedral. A local story, published in 1899, concerns a 'flying' cat photographed by G W French of Church Street.

 A few doors down is another ex-hostelry, the **New Inn**. In 1842, it is recorded that the landlord was Lacy Collard (1802-93), not to be confused with the builder of Abbotsfield, Charles Lukey Collard. Lacy later became a police constable and, in retirement, a sanitary inspector. His duties would have included enforcing a Victorian by-law 'requiring occupiers of premises to sweep adjoining footways daily before 9 a.m.'.

Tucked in behind and out of sight is **Ophir House**. Was this named for the Old Testament references to a city of gold, or because it was located on Golden Hill? It was built by the stalwart Methodist Nurcombe family, on the site of the first Wesleyan Chapel in the town (registered as such in 1837). The congregation grew sufficiently that a new chapel was built in South Street in 1845.

Ophir House

On the right as we descend the hill is a block of tenements, known as **Sunny Bank**, but also (by some) as 'The Barracks'. The then new buildings are believed to have housed a Volunteer Corps of troops, recruited in 1803 during the Napoleonic Wars. They were later described as Brewer's Cottages and, in 1936, were condemned. However, during the 1939-45 War they were used as billets and in 1970 their potential was spotted. They were modernised into attractive town houses with unusual oriel windows.

Golden Hill 'barracks'

WATER HYDRANTS

In the wall between Nos. 22 and 24 a small archway records one of eighteen hydrants planned for installation in 1866 when the first public piped water was laid into the town from Farmers Cleave. In varying states of preservation, the inscription reads

T. KENNEDY, PATENTEE, KILMARNOCK

SURVIVING EXAMPLES

8 Golden Hill (arch only)

Between 22 and 24 Golden Hill ('The Barracks')

Newgate Lane (half-way along on the up-hill side)

Junction of Golden Hill & Burges Close (re-sited)

Style Lane (opposite the Gas Factory)

North Street (wall below Richard Beadon Close)

White Horse Mews (on the left)

West Street, at The Larder (arch only)

Rotten Row (the Old School building)

Church Street, at 'Old Cottage'

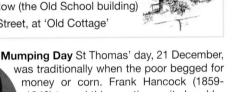

Mumping Day St Thomas' day, 21 December, was traditionally when the poor begged for money or corn. Frank Hancock (1859-1943) turned this practice on its head by being dropped at the bottom of Golden Hill. He would walk up, as a contemporary account recalled: 'giving each woman at the door of her cottage a half-crown for which she would curtsey, while the menfolk touched a forelock'.

Frank Hancock

The Bakery shopfront was extended after a fire in the 1930s

No. 35, the shop on the corner of Golden Hill and Newgate Lane, was one of the oldest bakeries in the town until it closed at Christmas time 1976. In an 1803 survey of stocks and supplies during the Napoleonic wars, the eight Wiveliscombe bakers stated they normally produced 1,580 3-lb loaves every twenty-four hours, which could be increased to 2,140 in an emergency.

The turn into **Newgate Lane** from Golden Hill for a car is dauntingly difficult. On the uphill side, there is a

good view of Ophir House. There are some pretty cottages in this narrow street. An old dye-works at the far end of the lane was used for accommodation during the 1939-45 War, although condemned on account of damp. The northern of the two cottages had been a wash house.

Newgate Lane, 1933

Masons Square

Masons Square was a courtyard on the right at the foot of Golden Hill, and home to ten families. It was demolished in 1963, and replaced by three bungalows. The white house ahead was once a farm called Style.

Foot of Golden Hill showing Masons Square and the gas-holder

As you turn left into Style Road (previously Muddy Lane) almost immediately on the right is a footpath called **Cut-throat Lane**, which strikes north down the valley towards Ford. A felon is reputed to have cleaned his knife here after a stabbing.

Next was the site of the Wiveliscombe Gas Light & Coke Co (of which only the house remains). It began in 1857 when the town was the smallest in England to have its own gas works. The undertaking was absorbed by the Taunton company in 1936 and the gas-holder here was demolished in 1964. The Brewery also installed its own gas works in 1905, thereby saving about 80% of their previous bills.

The 1960s **Style Road flats** look across to the Rugby club's second pitch, which was opened in 1983, and the Plain Pond allotments. As the road widens out, an old footpath on the left leads up to the North Street car park, passing the western ends of the burgage plots on Golden Hill.

Beyond **Spring Gardens** (early 1970s bungalows), is **Bolloms Mead**, built in 1985 on part of the Clatworthy House allotments and Mr Brown's market garden. **Lister House** on the corner was opened in 1986, to replace the surgery on Town Hill with the '1804' sign.

Opposite is **Northgate**, built in two phases in the 1920s and 1930s. **Plain Pond** and the **Allenslade Flats**, to the north, were also built for the Council between 1946 and 1948. The more recent, 2008, **Allenslade Close**, is a mixture of rented and shared-equity dwellings. What remains of the stone wall on the eastern side of the road to Langley Cross was built at the end of the 1939-45 War by prisoners-of-war.

Overlooking this end of the town is **Greenway Farm**, built in 1848 by Charlie Hayes for the Boucher family. At **Greenway Cottage** a lane rises steeply towards Maundown, meeting Jews Lane at a junction reputed to be haunted by the ghost of Tytibye. He was buried at this remote spot as the law then banned suicides from churchyard interment.

Northgate and Plain Pond

Northgate looking towards the Gasworks

Heading back towards The Square, **Tuckers Meadow**, on the right, is a group of bungalows for elderly people, opened by the local MP, Jeremy Browne, in September 2006. Next on the west side of the road are several Victorian-period public buildings.

Evacuee children gathered at Croford for their 2km walk to school

The **Primary School** building dates from 1877, when the National School moved up from the building near the parish church and became the Board School. It was renamed Wiveliscombe Council School in 1903 and taught all-age pupils until 1953 when Kingsmead Secondary School was opened. Numbers swelled during the 1939-45 War when 120 evacuees came from London. In January 1967, W J (Bill) Corney, headmaster from 1941-69, published a comprehensive monograph *Education in Wiveliscombe 1835-1966*.

Primary School pre-1923

The flêche was lost in a fire in 1923

Opposite the school **Pulsford Lodge** is a residential home for the elderly, opened in 1972, on the site of the Travellers Rest Inn which had been demolished c. 1920. *Bragg's Directory 1840* commented that the town was noted for the longevity of its residents, a feature which continues today.

Travellers' Rest

GINNETT'S Cirque Nationale,
WITH A SPLENDID STUD OF
50 HORSES & 50 ARTISTS.
FOR ONE DAY ONLY.

SATURDAY APRIL 29,

FIRST PERFORMANCE AT TWO P.M.; SECOND AT HALF-PAST SEVEN.
Prices:—First Class, 3s.; Second 1s.; Third 6d.; Schools Admitted at Half-price.

CEILING WALKER

Ginnett's Circus 1854

In part, Pulsford Lodge occupies a portion of the 'circus field', where visiting circuses were pitched. Residents still recall the Hancocks' benevolence in giving the 6d entrance fee to each of the small children queuing for a performance. Anderton & Rowland's fairground was evacuated to this field from Bristol during the 1939-45 War. Their Saturday afternoon performances are still remembered in the town.

The foundations of the chalet bungalow **Bowlyn** opposite were dug on 15 August 1952, the day of the Lynmouth flood disaster. The small building below, most recently a wine shop, was built in 1975, by undertaker Stan Shopland as a Chapel of Rest.

The **Police Station and Court** served Wiveliscombe, Milverton and a number of outlying villages. The Magistrate's Court next door closed in 1956 and the buildings were converted

Police Station

Police Cells

into dwellings in 1979. Adjacent, on the town side, two new police houses and a police office were constructed in the 1960s, all of which closed in 1995.

The **Fire Station** was built in the 1960s when the Brigade moved from their previous site opposite the rear entrance of the White Hart. Always a volunteer force, they have answered calls for assistance from as far away as Lynmouth, during the floods in 1952, a crashed aircraft on Maundown in 1943 and more recent incidents on the M5 motorway.

Fire Crew (1939-45 War)

*Spring Gardens
painted by W J Poole*

Stockers Close, built on the site of four dwellings, a linhay and orchard, recalls the town's links with the woollen trade. Joseph and Amos Stocker of a Quaker family were 17th and 18th century mercers, *i.e.* wool textile dealers.

On higher ground opposite is **Richard Beadon Close**. Three generations of that family, and that name, had connections with the town in the 19th century; as Bishop who owned the manor; his son who purchased much of the town in 1827; and grandson who was absentee Rector for forty-four years. The field was a 'rack close', where wool cloth was pegged out to be stretched and dried after fulling and bleaching.

Stocker Trade Token

Richard A'Court Beadon and his grandfather, the Bishop.

When the first plans for building the railway were drawn up in 1845, it was proposed that the station would be on the site of the **car park**. The plans were modified before construction began in the 1860s, and the area continued as a farmyard occupied by Bill Baker.

North Street, site of car park

Bill Baker and Riley Salter with putt cart 1937

North Street

The garage of **Rackleighs**, the large white house on the left where the Lutleys lived during the 19th century, was the fire station until the 1960s. The **Garden Shop** was previously a garage, which had replaced condemned cottages in 1948. Over the years there have been a variety of businesses between here and The Square, including four licensed premises: the King's Arms, the Bear, the White Horse and The Five Bells, the only survivor being the **Bear Inn**, believed to be the oldest in the town and dating from the 17th century.

White Horse Mews leads down behind this range of buildings to the site of the old cattle market, on much of which the Market Place houses have been built. Monthly markets were held here from 1889 when William Hancock II sold land behind his home, Court House, to the market committee. Some 50,000 sheep and 9,000 cattle passed under the hammer in 1900 but, by the 1960s, sales had dwindled, the last taking place in April 1984. A good example of

Red Devon Bulls

changing usage is demonstrated by the NatWest Bank, which replaced Mrs Merchant's shop, which in turn had been the White Horse Inn.

Wiveliscombe Great Market

THE Advantage which will be derived from a MARKET in the Town of WIVELISCOMBE, in the County of Somerset, for BULLOCKS, SHEEP, and other CATTLE, are so obvious, that from henceforth such MARKET will be kept, Four Times in every Year, on the following Days, viz.
THE LAST TUESDAY in FEBRUARY,
THE LAST TUESDAY in MARCH,
TRINITY TUESDAY, (instead of the Fair heretofore kept on *Trinity Monday*)
AND THE SECOND TUESDAY in DECEMBER.
☞ The FIRST MARKET to be on the LAST TUESDAY in the present Month of FEBRUARY.
WIVELISCOMBE, 4th February 1793.

Printed by PILES, BOOK-BINDERS, &c, NORTON.

Market Poster 1793

Mrs Mary Ann Merchant

White Horse Mews on the left

Opposite the Bear Inn, No. 3, was F J Hawkins, one of four butchers in the town at the turn of the century. He moved to West Street in 1920. Tom Stevens, who was severely wounded in the 1914-18 War,

F J Hawkins, North Street

established **Stevens Hair Fashions** in 1924 in Church Street. In 1934, he moved to this shop which had been occupied by watchmaker J H Stacey since the 1890s.

North Street looking to The Square

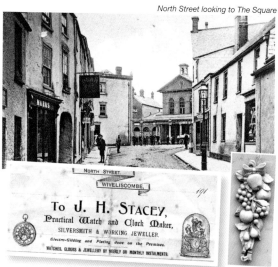

NORTH STREET,
WIVELISCOMBE,
191

To J. H. STACEY,
Practical Watch and Clock Maker,
SILVERSMITH & WORKING JEWELLER,
Electro-Gilding and Plating done on the Premises.
WATCHES, CLOCKS & JEWELLERY BY WEEKLY OR MONTHLY INSTALMENTS.

There is a fine choice of refreshments in The Square before we enter **West Street**, with shops on either side, but which was once a major thoroughfare, indeed it used to be the main road to North Devon.

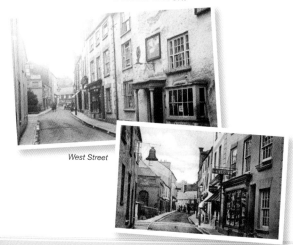
West Street

The Croft was the 19th century home of the Bouchers, a family of yeoman farmers, some of whom were also local lawyers. The eastward extension of 1832 was purchased by Hawkins the butcher when he moved from North Street in 1920. The same line of business has continued under different owners, and it is now the award-winning family-run **Thorne's Butchers**.

The **Jubilee Gardens** were opened in 1977 by Sir Henry F C Farrington Bt in commemoration of H M Queen Elizabeth II's Silver Jubilee, replacing a number of businesses, several of which are recalled in the gates designed by Steve Joyce in 2004 as part of the Wiveliscombe Heritage Arts Trail (WHAT) project. In 2012, Sir Henry W Farrington Bt unveiled a new plaque to commemorate the Queen's Diamond Jubilee.

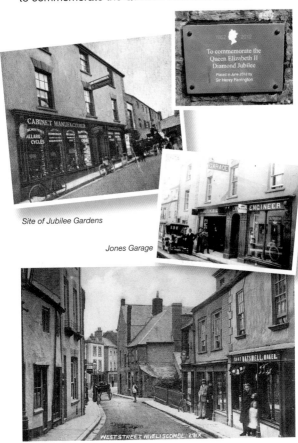

Site of Jubilee Gardens

Jones Garage

West Street

One of the row of shops had contained E J Thorne's emporium, *house furnishers, cabinet maker, pianoforte and china and glass dealers and cycle and phonograph agents, established in 1750*, which moved to Court House in The Square about the time of the 1914-18 War. Thorne's old premises became a garage, run first by Allan Hatswell, followed by Leonard Jones, and then various other trades before demolition in 1965.

The **Spar Shop** and **Wivey Hardware** were both part of Richards Brothers' Stores founded in 1857, still retaining similar trades as in the 19th century: *i.e.* bakery and confectionary, and household and ironmongery. County Stores operated in what is now the **Spar Shop** from 1925 to 1969, where children bought penny buns on their way to school.

Richards' Bakery West Street

Richards' Bag

County Stores

The **Post Office**, with its distinctive geometric frieze, was once the George Inn (after relocation from the mews on the north side of The Square). In 1827 a mail coach en route from Bristol via Taunton to Barnstaple called at the Lion Inn on Town Hill, close to where the town's Postmaster, one of the Hancock's, operated until 1860. By 1872 the Post Office was at 12 West Street and moved to No. 14 in 1925. The opening of the railway brought the telegraph in 1871, followed by the telephone c.1909.

Post Office c.1933

The Larder was previously a cobbler's and shoe shop belonging to George Slocombe and more recently Jim Adams. At one time the building had been the Salvation Army Citadel and behind was a smithy. **No. 24** was built in the 1930s by 'Doc' Edward Hall as his home and veterinary surgery, replacing a row of cottages.

Quarry Cleeve

Pulsford's Albion Lorry c.1937

At the foot of Jews Lane was the home of Ivor (Bug) Burston, the author of *Wiveliscombe 'Bits and Pieces' 1920's-1980's*, published in 1983. The lane leads up to the late 18th century racecourse on the top of Maundown, passing three substantial houses. First comes **Storey's Close**, named after a long-standing local family who established a charity for the parish poor in 1648. It was the home of George Frankau and his niece, the children's author, M E Atkinson (1899-1974). **Kingsmead** was built by Herbert Hancock in 1912. It was the home of local solicitor Arthur Tucker Pearse, who bequeathed money for a new pavilion on the recreation ground in 1930. Sydney Pulsford (1901-69) local haulier, businessman, parish, district and county councillor, also lived there. Local legend recalls a white line being painted on the road down to the town to assist Sydney when his eyesight failed. The stable block has recently been developed as a separate residence. The furthest house in Jews Lane, **Quarry Cleeve**, was built in 1906 for Froude Hancock (1865-1933) and his wife Violet. The thatch was replaced by slates after a fire in 1926. Alp's Quarry forms part of the garden.

West Street becomes West Road at **Westwayne**, another Boucher property previously called Old World House, and before that, Saunders. Opposite is **Jones' Garage**, built on the site of a malt-house and cottage in 1936 by Leonard Jones when he moved a short distance up from West Street.

On the right were the Webber's smithy and Mount Farm dairy, into which cows were walked for milking until the mid-1970s. Behind these buildings, a leat ran to supply water to the town. In this area it is believed there were once small dye mills.

'West End' Smithy

On the south side is the 17th century **Sharpe House**, one of the few buildings in town to retain its original name. Over time home to the Boucher, Chorley, Hancock and Lutley families and, more recently, the late Rear Admiral G S Ritchie, CB, DSC, Hydrographer of the Navy 1966-71. The house now provides sheltered accommodation for adults.

One of the attractive houses, **No. 8** with the balcony, facing the Recreation Ground, was the home of Mrs Eva Hyatt, the eldest daughter of G W French, the photographer of Church Street. Of five boys and seven girls, only she, and her fourth sister, Hildred, who continued the family boot and shoe business in Church Street, remained in the town.

French family house

Major Edward Driver lived in **Alpine House**; as manager of the local bank he was able to store the Home Guard ammunition in the Bank vaults. **Auckland Villa, No. 12**, home of the Hatswell family, was one of the properties built in the 1840s by Charles Hayes.

Delivery cart in West Road

Abbotsfield Cottages

Abbotsfield Cottages, built for Charles Lukey Collard in 1875 on the site of the demolished Bampton Inn, were for his outdoor staff at Abbotsfield.

Beside the garage, Weare Lane leads to **Farmers Cleave** passing **Alps Quarry**, now landscaped within private gardens. The quarry supplied much of the stone used to rebuild the parish church in 1827. The lane leads along a chestnut avenue to the old reservoir which supplied the town's water until the 1950s. The quarry manager lived in **West Weare**, built by the Nurcombe family, who also converted **West Weare Cottage** from a store into a house. **Redcliffe** was a private maternity home and kindergarten run by Nurse Prout (1876-1940, née Alice Maude Nusser) whose husband Edward was a partner in Doble and Prout, outfitters, in The Square. There are still residents of the town who were born at Redcliffe.

On the site of an old turnpike toll-house, was the town's first garage, Hatswell's; Allan and his son, also Allan, were there for over forty years after moving from West Street in 1922. Ronald Harvey and Archdale Walker had started the

Widows 'Penny'

business in 1910 but both were killed in action in the 1914-18 War and are commemorated on the same tablet in the parish church.

Hatswell's Garage, previously a smithy

Garage foundation

The footpath ends at the garage, the road is narrow and overhung with trees but behind, to the north, is the private fifty-acre Abbotsfield estate, purchased in 1870 from Samuel Lutley. Charles Lukey Collard (1806-91), from an old Langley family, owner of a successful pianoforte-making business in London, had planned an expensive mansion. It is not known why the attic rooms are directly over the ground floor rooms giving it an ill-proportioned appearance.

Charles Lukey Collard 1806-91

The orangery on the south wing has been demolished and, in the 1950s, the house and outbuildings were converted into a number of flats. The Collard name lives on in an annual music fellowship awarded by the Worshipful Company of Musicians in the name of John Clementi Collard, the second of Lukey's four sons.

Abbotsfield with Orangery

A spring beside the Abbotsfield Lodge supplied the brewery and higher up the hill were the 17th century Colles almshouses, demolished in 1897. In the fields

Abbotsfield ballroom

on the south side mules, imported from overseas for work with the Army, were grazed during the 1914-18 War.

Mules arriving at the Station

Three private houses on the hill are Deane View, built on land within the Prebendal estate; Culverhead, with a landscaped park, built in the 1890s for Froude and Violet Hancock, who moved to Quarry Cleeve in 1906, and Culverhead Lodge, just west of the tennis courts, which has a Nissen hut in the garden, all that remains of an American war-time camp. Latvian refugees lived in the camp until 1952.

Latvians

Wartime GIs

1914-18 War Memorial

The **Recreation Ground**, '**The Rec**', previously called Broad Meadow, was purchased by the town in 1919 from John Tidboald, who farmed at nearby Culverhay. The field was dedicated as a perpetual amenity memorial for the 1914-18 War on 3 June 1920. The obelisk was made from stone quarried at Ford. Nearby is a 1939-45 War memorial drinking fountain.

1939-45 War Memorial

Maypole dance 1934

Festival tableau reflecting a popular 1960's TV show

Broad Meadow had been used for shows such as the 1902 Somerset County Agricultural Association and, from 1912, the Wiveliscombe Horticultural Society. In 1975 the latter moved to Kingsmead School, where annually nearly forty cups are still competed for in various classes, not only fruit and vegetables, but also floral art, cookery, home-made wines and handicrafts. As well as such events as the annual town bonfire and fireworks, the main use of 'The Rec' remains for sport.

Agricultural Show 1902

Horticultural show, 1947

The ground is much used for swimming, tennis, cricket and rugby and, more recently, a skate board facility has been erected. An anonymous Scottish visitor to the town was heard to remark: 'Where I come from Rugby is a sport - down here it is a religion'. So it has been since the 1870s when the game was introduced by an engineer, F L J Rooke (1852-75), engaged in building the railway.

The club is the second oldest in Somerset. It has produced both county and international players, and the invention of the four man three-quarter line is credited to Francis 'Frank' E Hancock (1859-1943), one of seven rugby playing sons of William and Mary Hancock. On 11 April 1935, T Vincent Pearse opened a 'new' pavilion, funded by a legacy from his brother Arthur Pearse. The clubhouse was opened in 1967 and extended ten years later, followed by recent work in 2012.

WRFC 1901-02

TV Pearse opening
the pavilion 1935

Pool Opening 4/8/1927

The 'Rec' 1920s

Hancock memorial shelter 1934

The swimming pool, built in 1927 by the builder William White, was supplied by water from the Withycombe reservoir in Farmers Cleave. Since installation of heating in 1995 and subsequent refurbishment, it has become very popular. The grass tennis courts, laid a few years earlier, were surfaced in the 1980s. Next to the tennis courts is a shelter erected to the memory of Philip Froude Hancock (1865-1933), another of the seven rugby playing Hancock brothers. He was capped by England four times and played on the first British Lions tour of South Africa (1891).

Old views show the unique row of pollarded fir trees which disappeared when Croft Way was constructed in 1980. Built to relieve serious congestion in the town on the then main road into North Devon, only one building had to be demolished.

One house demolished

Invitation to the opening

> *They are arguing over a bypass,*
> *The juggernauts plough up the road,*
> *We are trying to cross to the Co-op.*
> *Wait! Here comes a thirty-ton load.*
>
> Unattributed poem,
> *Wiveliscombe: A History* p.205

The **Children's Society Centre**, on the south side of the road, opened in May 2008, provides facilities for up to forty-five youngsters.

At the eastern end of the public **car park**, a path climbs towards West Street passing the **Community Centre.** This had been the stables of the Bell Inn (now London House) which were converted for use by the local Conservative Association in the 1920s and named the Constitutional Rooms. In the 1930s, the Women's Institute took over the management and they continue to hold a monthly market in the Hall. When the need for a community building was identified in the late 1970s, money was raised to purchase the property for the town. Now known as the Community Centre, it was opened on 8 May 1982 by the local MP, The Rt Hon. Edward du Cann.

The Diamond Garden
To Commemorate the Diamond Jubilee Of Her
Majesty Queen Elizabeth II
1952 - 2012

Officially opened by Mrs Jean Holland
2nd June 2012

Congratulations from your
loyal Subjects of
Wiveliscombe

Attached to the east wall is a 2012 Diamond Jubilee commemorative plaque overlooking a small newly created garden. On the right is the studio of the local '10Radio' station which first broadcast in 2005. This is one of a number of innovative organisations in the town established over the past ten years. Others include the biennial Ten Parishes Festival, which highlights artistic talent in the neighbourhood, the local newspaper the *Wiveliscombe Messenger*, printed and published in alternate months by the *West Somerset Free Press* on behalf of the Wiveliscombe Civic Society, and the Wiveliscombe Area Partnership, which provides support to community and business endeavours in the town.

On reaching **The Square** you may encounter any manner of events: the Remembrance Day parade, a meet of the hounds on Boxing Day, market stalls, Father Christmas. Tony Hill, bearing the torch he carried earlier in the summer when he participated in the Olympic Torch Relay, led the 2012 Carnival Procession through The Square. Many occasions are enhanced by the Town Band which dates from 1896, and has been an integral part of the social life of the community ever since.

Hounds meet in The Square

Town Band

Tony Hill

Dear Wilscombe,
may your beauteous lanes and hills
Resound with happy music and with glee;
And England's gracious land and rippling rills,
Be thankful unto God, for such as thee.

Chas. Collard 11th November 1936

Bibliography

Ashburton, Lord *The Somersetshire Estates of the Right Honourable Lord Ashburton* 1894 [SHC A\AGI/1/37]

Batey, Stanley *Forerunner of the Welfare State? The Public Dispensary and Infirmary of 1804* (1978) Wiveliscombe Historical Society ISBN 0904412016

Batey, Stanley *The Provident Society of 1810* (1981) Wiveliscombe Historical Society ISBN 0904412024

Batey, Stanley *Wiveliscombe Celebrations 1897-1953* (nd) Wiveliscombe Historical Society

Beadon, Richard *Particulars and Conditions of Sale of the Wiveliscombe Estate ... 15 September 1834* [SHC D/HCK/10/1/7]

Beadon, Richard *The Particulars of the Wiveliscombe and Fitzhead Estate ... 13 and 14 September 1838* [SHC DD/X/WHS/2/5]

Bodman, Martin *Mills Around Wiveliscombe* (2000) SIAS Survey No. 12 ISBN 0953353915

Bragg, William *General Directory for the County of Somerset* (1840)

Burston, Ivor *Bits and Pieces 1920's-1980's* (1983) Author

Clark, F Graham *A Somerset Life, An Account of the Business Career of Mrs B A Langdon of Wiveliscombe* (c.1957) Langdon & Sons Ltd

Collingridge, Brian *A Short History of Kingsmead School* (2003) Author

Collinson, John *The History and Antiquities of the County of Somerset* (1791)

Collinson-Morley, Kathleen *The History of the Brendon Hills, Tiverton, Bampton, Milverton and Wiveliscombe* (nd) Cox & Sons, Minehead

Corney, W G *Education in Wiveliscombe 1835-1966* (1967) Author

English Heritage Website *British Listed Buildings, ID 270202* (1975)

Farrington, Susan Maria *Sancti Stones* (2001) Colden Publications ISBN 0954099206

Farrington, Susan Maria and The Wiveliscombe Book Group Wiveliscombe: *A History of a Somerset Market Town* (2005) Colden Publications ISBN 0954099214

Gledhill, David *The Gas Works of Somerset* (2003) SIAS ISBN 0953353974

Hancock, Reverend Frederick *Wifela's Combe: A History of the Parish of Wiveliscombe* (1911) Barnicott and Pearce, Taunton

Holder, R W *Taunton Cider and the Langdons: A West Somerset Story of Industrial Development* (2000) Phillimore & Co. ISBN 1860771378

Kelly's Directories Ltd *Directory of Somerset* (Various editions 1861-1939)

Lyddon, W J *A Guide to the Parish Church of St Andrew, Wiveliscombe* (1955)

Marshall, Revd C J B St Andrew's, *Wiveliscombe: Its Bells, Ringers and Ringing* (1980)

McCririck, Revd Howard *A Sketch of the History of Wiveliscombe Parish Church* (Revised 1938)

Miles, Mary *Hancock's Brewery Wiveliscombe* (1985) SIAS Survey No. 2 ISBN 0950977616

Peppard, Nesta *Bygone Wiveliscombe from the pictorial archive of Nesta Peppard* (2009) DVD and CD

Slaters (late Pigot & Co) *Royal National and Commercial Director and Topography 1852-3*

Somerset County Gazette (various dates)

Taunton Courier (various dates)

Vickery, John *Vickery's Illustrated Almanack, Diary and Wiveliscombe Directory for the Year 1908*

Villar, William J & Co. *Court House, Wiveliscombe Commodious Residence … Particulars* (1912)

Waldron, Clement "Some Account of the Town and Parish of Wiveliscombe" in *Proceedings SANHS* (1883, Vol.29, No.1)

Wellington Weekly News (various dates)

Wiveliscombe Messenger (various editions)

Wiveliscombe Parish Council *Wiveliscombe Circular Walks* (2006) ISBN 9780955285100

Wiveliscombe Parish Map Group Wiveliscombe *'Of Bishops, brewers and beasts'* (2002) Video

10Radio *Do Dormice Live Here? Seven Wildlife Walks Around Wiveliscombe* (2011) CD

Index

*Designed by
Will Glanfield*

*Designed by
Steve Joyce*

*Designed by
John Alder*

Acknowledgements and Credits

All those who so generously gave their time or contributed in any way to *Wiveliscombe: A History* may justifiably feel they have a share in this sequel. There is also no doubt that without the legacy of those who have gone before, our knowledge and understanding of Wiveliscombe would be greatly diminished.

Especial thanks to Diana Farrington for the line-drawings and maps, and to all those who have loaned photographs, particularly Nesta Peppard, whose collection of town images is exceeded by none. We are grateful for the input of local historians Bob Croft and Dixon Luxton, and to Glenda Anderson, Frankie Dransfield and Katriona Smith for help in preparing the text for publication.

It has been a pleasure working with Steve Farthing (Legend Design) and Mark Couch and his team at Short Run Press.

Illustrations

The following have kindly agreed to the use of images in their possession for which we are very grateful:

Jim Adams
John Alder
Jean Baker
Tony Bishop
David Bond
Adrienne Broom
Ronald Chown
Brian Collingridge
Bob Croft
Frankie Dransfield
Diana Farrington
Mrs M G Foxwell
Godfrey Fry
Phil Gadd
Edith Gear
Judith Greedy
Pam Griffiths
Richard Grylls
Peter Hancock
William Hancock
Jane Hawkins
Allan & Rosalie Hughes
Malcolm & Pauline Hurd
Geoffrey Jones
Cheryl Kehyaian

Dixon Luxton
Dave Meehan
Hilary Miller
Dick Moody
Mary Nation
Richard Northey
Nesta Peppard
Jim Pincombe
George Potter
John & Edwina Pugsley
Derrick Pulsford
Valerie Read
John Rees
Bernadette Rowe
Riley Salter
Ann Scotter
Sue Solomon
Lil Stone
Simon Turnbull
Martin Valuks
Betty Webber
Gordon White
Jim Whyatt
Jean Woodbury

We also acknowledge, with thanks,
specific permissions from:

Bellwood Photography

Wiveliscombe Horticultural Society Show, 1947

Museum of English Rural Life, University of Reading

Thorne Brothers tailors' label

Sir Alfred Munnings Art Museum

'Wings for Victory Week' cartoon

Somerset Archive & Local Studies Service *[SHC]*

Wiveliscombe Town Map 1816 *SHC A\ACD/1*
Ashburton Sale Catalogue 1894 *SHC A\AGI/1/37*
1841 Wiveliscombe Town Map *SHC D\D/Rt/M/355*
Frank Hancock *SHC A\AGI/1/12*
Mules at the railway station *SHC A\AGI/1/40*

Somerset Museums Service [SMS]

Wiveliscombe Bank £5 note *SMS 222/1988/159*
Hancock Bottle *SMS 76.A1.205*
Stocker Token *SMS OS.AC.1288*

Wifela's Combe

Old Market House
Old St Andrew's church

Wiveliscombe Heritage Art Trail (WHAT)

John Alder:	Bristol Inn, Green Dragon, Lion Hotel, Noahs Ark
Joanna Dewfall:	Swan, The Anchor,
Michael Fairfax:	Kings Arms
Bronwen Gwillim:	New Inn, Royal Oak, The Bell
David Reeves:	White Horse Inn
Julia Smith:	Black Dog, Borough Inn
Will Spankie:	George Inn, Masons Arms

Wiveliscombe Rugby Football Club (WRFC)

WRFC 1901-2 Season team photograph

GREETINGS FROM
Wiveliscombe

General View of Wiveliscombe.

North Street.